You should b
picking up a

Also available from Sphere Books:

RUGBY JOKES
RUGBY SONGS
MORE RUGBY SONGS
SON OF RUGBY JOKES
MORE RUGBY JOKES
EVEN MORE RUGBY JOKES
RUGBY JOKES SCORE AGAIN

WHAT RUGBY JOKES DID NEXT

What Rugby Jokes Did Next

SPHERE HUMOUR CLASSICS

SPHERE BOOKS LIMITED

SPHERE BOOKS LTD

Published by the Penguin Group
27 Wrights Lane, London W8 5TZ, England
Viking Penguin Inc., 40 West 23rd Street, New York, New York 10010, USA
Penguin Books Australia Ltd, Ringwood, Victoria, Australia
Penguin Books Canada Ltd, 2801 John Street, Markham, Ontario, Canada L3R 1B4
Penguin Books (NZ) Ltd, 182–190 Wairau Road, Auckland 10, New Zealand

Penguin Books Ltd, Registered Offices: Harmondsworth, Middlesex, England

First published in Great Britain by Sphere Books Ltd 1970
Reprinted 1971, 1972, 1976, 1978, 1979, 1981 (twice), 1982,
1984, 1985, 1987, 1988

Printed and bound in Great Britain by
Cox & Wyman Ltd, Reading
Set in Intertype Baskerville

THIS IS A CHAIN LETTER

Dear Friend:
This chain was started in the hope of bringing happiness to all tired business men. Unlike most chains, it doesn't require money. Simply send a copy of this to five male friends, then bundle up your wife and send her to the fellow whose name heads the list. When your name reaches the top of the list, you will receive 15,186 women and some should be corkers. Have faith. Don't break the chain. One man broke it and got his wife back.

Your friend,
Homebreakers, Ltd.

FLAT OUT

A young lady was permitted by her parents to take employment in a large city and live in her own apartment. The one condition was that she would not allow gentlemen friends to her flat as it would worry her mother.

During a long distance phone conversation, the daughter described her date of the previous evening to her mother.

"You didn't permit that man in your flat, did you?" queried the nervous mother.

"Oh, no!" replied the daughter, "we went to his flat. Let his mother worry."

CARRY ON FIREMAN

John, a 6ft. 2in. fireman from Yorkshire, thought he had every reason to be pleased with the results of his first evening out in London. After a few pints at the pub, here he was bedded down with a delightful redhead whom he hadn't known for longer than an hour.

Unfortunately those pints at the pub (not to mention the chasers in between) had a rather softening effect on his otherwise passionate advances. Hoping that his customary vigour would return to him later in the evening, John tried to make conversation:

"I'm a big fireman from Bradford," he told her.

"Well," replied the redhead, "either start paying out more hose, or get closer to the fire!"

FAT WOMAN TO FAT MAN

"Thanks for the tip."

A ROSE BY ANY OTHER NAME

Harold and Mabel were admiring the view from the window of their honeymoon hotel. Slightly flushed with embarrassment Mabel turned to her newly acquired husband and asked :

"Harold, darling, now that we're married at last, please tell me : what is a penis?"

Delighted by her innocence, Harold led her back into the bedroom, took off his trousers and showed her.

"Oh!" she exclaimed, "It's just like a prick, only smaller."

THE ULTIMATE INSULT

"Is it in?"

THE WAGES OF SIN

Three young boys were playing in the street of a London slum. A Rolls Royce stopped and a beautiful, expensively dressed blonde stepped out. She crossed over to the boys, picked up the youngest, hugged him and left a box of candies, and filled his hands with money. Waving goodbye, she re-entered the car and departed. The other boys were goggle-eyed.

One said, "Blimey, Jackie, was that yer fairy godmother?"

Jackie looked at him with scorn and replied, "Naw, that wuz my sister wot was ruined."

AFTERTHOUGHT

Bellhop at the 'Hit and Run' Hotel. "Anything else, sir . . . ?"

Man : "No, that's all. Thank you."

Bellhop : "Anything for your wife . . . ?"

Man : "Why, yes. Come to think of it. Bring me a post-card."

AN APPLE A DAY

Harry's sore throat was bothering him so much that he went along to the doctor's house at lunchtime, even though it was outside normal surgery hours.

The doorbell was answered by the doctor's pretty young wife.

"Is the doctor in?" Harry whispered hoarsely.

"He won't be back till three," she whispered back, "come on in."

THE HORSE'S MOUTH

Sally, a buxom young deb, had been out riding all morning and when she brought the horse back to the stable, it was tired out and lathered with sweat. As she dismounted the groom remarked:

" 'E looks just about done in."

"You'd be tired too," replied Sally, "if you'd been between my legs for as long as that horse has."

TIT FOR TEAT

Despite his good looks and his rich 600 acre farm, Fred had never managed to have his way with the buxom farmgirl who milked his cows. So he took her away to watch his prize bull servicing a cow, in the hope that the spectacle would set the juices churning in her ripe young body.

"Believe me," he told her as they watched, "I'd like to be doing what that bull is doing right now!"

"Why don't you?" she answered, "it's your cow."

A HARD DECISION

The party was in full flow when George set out on a tour of inspection round the house. In one of the bedrooms he came upon a naked girl fast asleep under an eiderdown. Unable to resist the temptation, he stripped off his own clothes, clambered aboard and began making love to her. She soon woke up and asked him what on earth he thought he was doing.

"Shall I take it out?" asked George.

"Take it out," she replied, "and then put it in again a few times so that I can make up my mind."

THE MARKET PRICE

Everyone looked up as the couple walked through the restaurant to their table. She was young, beautiful and voluptuous while he was old, haggard and stooped. The waiter came over to take their order and the young woman proceeded to order the most expensive dishes in the house. Her escort was somewhat staggered and asked, "Do you eat this well at home?"

"No," she replied, "but then, no one there wants to sleep with me!"

PLAYBACK

A bra manufacturer who sells his product under the slogan "Every Girl Wants EMBARGO" was asked why he picked "EMBARGO" for a trade name. "At first glance you may think it's foolish," he explained, "but spelled backwards, it has tremendous sales appeal."

A DISAPPOINTING SWEET

Mrs Jones was on trial for beating up her husband so badly that he had to spend two weeks in hospital.

On the night of the incident, her lawyer explained, Mrs Jones had locked her husband out of the bedroom because he was disgustingly drunk. But Mr Jones kept hammering on the door, saying:

"I bet you'd let me in if you knew what I was knocking with."

When she got up at once to unlock the door, he came in and gave her a box of chocolates.

FANCY UNDRESS

Fanny ransacked her wardrobe for something to wear at the Fancy Dress Ball. Finding nothing suitable she simply took off all her clothes and went along stark naked as Eve.

But the Doorman turned her away on the grounds that nudity didn't represent anybody in particular.

Twenty minutes later she was back, still naked except for a pair of black gloves and black shoes.

"Who are you supposed to be now?" asked the doorman, preparing to turn her away a second time.

"Can't you see?' answered Fanny, "I'm the five of spades."

BIRD TALK

Aunt Mildred decided to buy a parrot to keep her company. The local pet shop had a good selection, but one bird with bright green and blue feathers immediately caught her attention as the pick of the bunch. Curiously enough the shopkeeper seemed reluctant to sell it.

"I don't think he's really Madame's sort of parrot," he explained evasively.

"Why on earth not?"

"He doesn't come from a very nice home. Now, if madame would care to step this way, I think I have just the bird . . .'

"But I don't *like* any of those. I want this one," Mildred insisted.

"Very well, madam." Noting the glint of determination in Mildred's eye, the shopkeeper sold her the bird and an expensive wrought iron cage to go with it.

Mildred installed the parrot in her sitting room and waited breathlessly for his first words. The parrot flapped his wings, looked around the house and said:

"New house. Very nice."

Mildred was delighted.

At half past four Mildred's two teenage daughters came back from school. The parrot cocked an eye at them and said:

"New girls. Very nice."

Mildred clapped her hands with joy. Not only was the parrot such a magnificent specimen, but he had perfect manners. No wonder the man at the pet store hadn't wanted to part with him!

At half past five her husband Henry returned from the office. The parrot skittered to the front of his cage and said:

"New house. New girls. Same old customer. How are you Henry?"

A SNATCH OF CONVERSATION

Finding himself next to a rather striking mini-skirted blonde in the bus queue on a windy day, George decided to strike up a conversation with her.

"Airy, isn't it?" he remarked.

"Wot did yer hexpect," she answered haughtily, "hostrich feathers?"

CINEMATIC TECHNIQUE

On Saturday nights Tom and Hilda usually went to the pictures to pet in the back row. One night, when they were showing Dracula's Grave, Hilda's squeals and giggles of excitement attracted the attention of the Manager.

"What's the matter young lady?" he asked, "Are you feeling hysterical?"

"No, he's feeling mine."

QUESTIONS AND ANSWERS

Q. What do you call an uncircumcised Jewish baby?
A. A girl.

Q. What is a lesbian?
A. A mannish depressive with delusions of gender.

Q. What is a gynaecologist?
A. A spreader of old wives' tales.

Q. What's the difference between a vitamin and a hormone?
A. You can't hear a vitamin.

Q. What do you call an abortion in Prague?
A. A cancelled cheque.

Q. Why don't prostitutes vote?
A. Because they don't care who gets in.

Q. How do porcupines make love?
A. Very carefully.

HORSE SENSE

Said the worried patient to the psychiatrist: "I'm in love with my horse."

"But that's nothing," replied the psychiatrist. "A lot of people love animals. My wife and I have a dog that we love very much."

"Ah, but doctor, it's a physical attraction that I feel toward my horse!"

"Ummmm!" said the psychiatrist. "What kind of horse is it? male or female?"

"Female of course!" the gent shot back angrily. "What do you think I am, queer?"

UNDERSTATEMENT

A man called the undertaker and cried, "Come over and bury my wife."

"But," said the mortician, "I buried your wife ten years ago."

"I got married again," sobbed the man.

"Congratulations," said the undertaker.

A HEAVENLY REUNION

Elsie died at the age of ninety-two, having outlived a remarkable total of eight husbands. At the funeral one of her neighbours remarked : "At last they're together again."

"Which husband are you talking about?" asked another of the neighbours.

"I'm not talking about her husbands," came the reply, "I'm talking about her legs."

PASS THE BUCK

At dinner Daisy told her stodgy old husband about her visit to the doctor :

"When he examined me, he admired my breasts and said they were very beautiful."

"Did he," asked her husband, "say anything about your great fat arse?"

"No," answered Daisy. "I don't think he mentioned you at all."

A MATTER OF PRINCIPLE

A man was travelling to Manchester with his family by train. Since their compartment was a non-smoker, he went next door to smoke a cigar. The only other occupant was a rather dejected young man, gazing moodily out of the window. Harry offered him a cigar.

"No thank you," said the young man, "I don't smoke."

When Harry had finished with his newspaper, he asked the young man whether he'd like to read it.

"No thank you," he replied, "I don't read."

Still hoping to cheer up his travelling companion, Harry offered to buy him a drink.

"No thank you," came the refrain, "I don't drink."

Refusing to admit defeat, Harry tried again:

"Young man, I admire your principles. I'd like you to come and meet my wife and daughter in the next compartment."

"No thank you. I don't screw either."

LIKE FATHER, LIKE SON

George ran the business in partnership with his son. When his son showed signs of worry and strain, George asked him what the matter was, reminding him that, as partners, they must share their responsibilities.

"Well, Dad, since you put it that way, the typist is pregnant, and she wants *us* to marry her."

NIGHTRIDE

Making love on the backseat of the car, a young couple were interrupted by the arrival of a policeman.

"What are you doing in there?" asked the policeman.

"Just necking officer," replied the young man.

"Well put your neck back in your trousers, and drive on."

A NEW DEAL FOR YOUNG LOVERS

An Irish priest was disturbed by the number of women in his flock who confessed to him that they had been seduced by the grocer's new delivery boy. As a penance he asked them all to put ten shillings in the poor box. When the delivery boy came to make his confession, the priest asked angrily:

"Well, boy, what have you got to say for yourself?"

"Just this father," he replied, "either you give me a fair share of those ten shilling fees, or I take my business to the next parish."

MANSLAUGHTER

A couple, married for thirty years, had never missed a night of connubial bliss. Not feeling well one day, the wife consulted her doctor and was informed that she must have complete rest and quiet for six months or she would not live.

The wife and husband decided that they must stay completely apart during this period. She moved into an upstairs bedroom and he remained downstairs.

After three months of complete abstinence and solitude, his will power collapsed and he started for her bedroom. Just as he was about to ascend the stairs, he saw her coming down. Their eyes met and she said, "Dear, I was just coming down to die." To which he quickly replied, "I'm glad, darling, because I was just going up to kill you."

SAVED BY THE BELLE

A son comes to tell his father that he has got his girlfriend pregnant.

"How much do you need?" asks the father.

"A hundred and twenty pounds."

A few days later the second son arrives with the same story.

"How much?"

"A hundred and fifty pounds, Dad."

The next day the daughter comes and confesses that she is pregnant.

"Thank God," says the father, "business is looking up at last."

A SINNER PRAYS

Oh, Blessed Virgin we believe
That without sin thou didst conceive.
Teach us then how thus believing
We can sin without conceiving.

A LONELY DIET

The young bride asked her doctor for a simple and effective method of birthcontrol.

"Orange juice." he replied.

"Do you take it before or after?" asked the bride.

"Neither—instead."

DIVINE INTERVENTION

There was no doubt about it, Gloria was pregnant.

"Please feel free to use my telephone if you'd like to tell your husband," said the doctor.

"But doctor, I'm not married."

"Well, then, you'd better tell your lover."

"But I've never had a lover!"

"All right. Then I must ask you to go home and tell your mother to get ready for the second coming of Christ."

FAIL SAFE

After lights-out at an exclusive girls' school the conversation turned to the best method of avoiding pregnancy.

"My boy friend takes it out before he comes off," said the first girl, "but I know that's not very safe, so I'm going to get some pills during the holidays."

"I've been using the rhythm method," said the second, "but that means I can't have it very often. I think I'll go on the pill too."

"I wouldn't advise it," said the third, "I've tried and it keeps dropping out."

A SLIPPERY CUSTOMER

The chemist was trying to explain why this particular brand of contraceptive was so much more expensive than the rest.

"These ones," he said, "are guaranteed by the makers."

"But what if they break?"

"Then the guarantee runs out."

A SELLER'S MARKET

A man went into a chemists to find a cure for his persistent erection. He was embarrassed to find that there was only a female assistant, but she did her best to assure him that he could speak freely.

"Well, I've had this erection for two weeks, and I can't get it to go down. What can you give me for it?"

"Just a minute, please sir, I'd like to consult my partner."

The woman disappeared into the back of the shop and came back three minutes later.

"I've talked it over with my partner, and the best we can offer you is the shop and fifty pounds in cash."

GUESS AGAIN

It was at the office Christmas party. As they lay on the office reception couch in the darkened room, their breath came hot and fast.

"Oh, Melvin, Melvin," she said passionately, "you've never made love to me like this before. Is it because of the holiday spirit?"

"No" he panted. "It's probably because I'm not Melvin!"

PHOTO-PLAY

The husband finally cornered the Casanova who had been seducing his wife. "Look," he said, flourishing photos taken by a private detective he had employed. "Here's a shot of you and my wife in the living room of my apartment. Here's another of you drinking together, half undressed. And here's a picture of you two in bed together. Now, what are you going to do about it?"

The adulterer studied the photos carefully, nodding over each one. After a moment he picked up the third one and handed it to the husband. "All right," he said. "I'll take a dozen of this one."

HUMP-TY DUMP-TY

A man was walking down the street one afternoon when he was hit on the head by a used contraceptive thrown out of a second story window. Outraged, he pounded at the door of the offending house until the owner appeared.

"Whose window is that?" he asked, pointing to the second storey.

"My daughter's," replied the owner.

"Is she alone?"

"She's with my intended son-in-law, not that it's any of your business."

"Well in that case you might like to know that your intended grandson has just had a very bad fall."

CAUGHT IN THE ACT

Sally's mother, determined on a good marriage for her daughter, instructed her to let her rich boy friend have his way with her, and then, when he lit a cigarette afterwards, to say: "And what shall we call the baby?" He will then be forced to propose to her.

Sally did as she'd been told.

"If he gets out of that," said her boyfriend, throwing the contraceptive into the waste-paperbasket, "we'll call him Houdini."

A SALESMAN'S PITCH

A father of twins was pestered in the station waiting room by a nosey old lady who kept asking questions about his children. Every time she asked him a question, he would simply answer, "I don't know, Madam."

"How is it that you don't even know your own children's names, or whether they're boys or girls," the old lady asked.

"I'm not the father of these children, Ma'am," he answered, "I'm a contraceptive salesman, and these are two complaints I'm taking back to the factory."

CARNAL KNOWLEDGE

After a particularly enjoyable evening out, Susan asked Roger in for a cup of coffee in her parents' house.

Half an hour later her mother came down to find them having intercourse on the sofa. "Well I never . . ." she exclaimed.

"Don't be silly, mother," replied Susan, "of course you did."

THE NAME OF THE GAME

Three sisters were preparing to go out for the evening. All three went to say good-bye to their mother before they left.

"I'm going out with Pete to eat," said the first.

"That's nice, darling," said the mother, "try not to be late."

"I'm going out with Lance to dance," said the second.

"How lovely!" said the mother, "but do keep an eye on the time."

"I'm going out with Chuck," said the third.

"Oh, no you're not," said the mother, "you're staying right here."

ACROBATICS

The bride and groom realised from the sounds next door that the parents were listening through the wall. So they decided to pack up their belongings and move out to an hotel. Unaware of what was going on, the parents on the other side of the wall mistook the sounds of packing for the sounds of intercourse.

The hastily packed suitcase would not shut properly; "Let me sit on it," said the bride.

"No, I'll sit on it," whispered the groom.

"All right, let's both sit on it," said the bride.

At which point the father burst into the room, saying, "I'm sorry to interrupt, but this I've got to see!"

GENERATION GASP

The elderly gentleman was nearing eighty but refused to accept his loss of sexual desire and stamina. He consulted with his doctor.

The doctor was amused and asked "Why should you be so concerned? It's expected at your age."

"But," pursued the oldster, "a friend of mine who is eighty-five says he makes love to his wife every night."

The doctor smiled. "Well, can't you say the same thing?"

HAND OUT

Girl in theatre: "The man next to me is masturbating!"
Girl-friend: "Ignore him."
"I can't; he's using my hand!"

LISTEN WITH MOTHER

When their son brought his newlywed wife home for their first night together, Mr and Mrs Jones, eavesdropping from the next door bedroom, decided to do everything that the young couple did.

After the newlyweds had made love three times and were starting on number four, the father banged desperately on the wall and shouted :

"Tony, stop ! You're killing your mother !"

A NOTE ON THE BRIDAL BED

The cold cream's on the mantle
The shoe-horn's on the shelf;
I saw that great big thing of yours
And I chloroformed myself.

HANDY PANKY

A young couple travelled by train to their honeymoon hotel. During the journey the woman fondled her man under the cover of a newspaper spread across his lap. Later they both dozed off and a breeze blew the newspaper onto the floor. Then the conductor came by.

"Wake up, Madam," he said, shaking her awake. "Your bouquet has wilted."

WELL PRAYED!

The young vicar and his bride had just undressed and were ready to taste the fruits of love. But before the bride could clamber into the marital bed, he suggested they should kneel down together to pray for strength and guidance.

"Just pray for strength," said the bride. "I'll do the rest."

SHAFTED

Sally's girl-friend asked her to describe the first night of the honeymoon:

"All night it was up and down, in and out, up and down, in and out—our room was next to the lift."

ANIMAL INSTINCTS

Coming down to breakfast on the morning after the wedding night, the groom was surprised to find a fresh lettuce on his plate, and nothing else.

"What's this?" he asked.

"I just wanted to see whether you eat like a rabbit too," explained the bride.

TOO MANY COOKS...

A newly married couple were in Paris for their honeymoon. The groom went down to the lobby while his wife undressed upstairs, as she was still too shy to undress in his presence. Imagine his surprise when he came back to the suite ten minutes later to find her lying stark naked on the bed, copulating with one bellboy clutching the ardent members of two others in her hands and ministering to a fourth with her lips.

"Penelope!" cried the groom, "how *could* you?"

"Oh darling," she replied, releasing the fourth bellboy with an audible plop, "you know I've always been something of a flirt."

PUSH OVER

It was sundown, and the young athlete was doing push-ups on the beach when a drunk appeared. The drunk weaved his way to within a few yards of the perspiring young man, sat down on the sand and laughed and laughed. "What in the devil are you laughing about?" asked the annoyed young man. The drunk laughed and laughed, and then spluttered, "Don't look now, but shumbuddy sthole yur girl."

EYE WITNESS

Arriving home unexpectedly from a business trip, the husband found his wife in bed with his best friend, in what may be described as a compromising position.

"See here," shouted the husband, "just what do you two think you're doing?"

"See!" said the wife to the man beside her. "Didn't I tell you he was stupid?'

THE CROWN JEWELS

The groom stood naked in front of the mirror admiring his physique:

"Two inches more and I'd be a king."

"Yes," said the bride, "and two inches less and you'd be a queen."

SIZING OFF

The judge granted them a decree nisi.

As she left the courtroom, the wife turned to her ex-husband, waggled her little finger at him and called out: "Goodbye, Shorty.'

The man stretched the corners of his mouth with two fingers and replied: "Goodbye, Lucy."

THE THEORY OF RELATIVITY

Despite George's reputation as the office Romeo, the new secretary was not impressed by his performance.

"I don't think much of your organ," she said as she retrieved her panties from the IN tray.

"No?" replied George, "well I didn't expect to play in an auditorium."

DRIVING LICENCE

Three weeks before the birth of her firstborn, Lady Caroline paid a visit to her gynaecologist in Harley Street.

"What position," she inquired, "will I have to lie in to give birth to my baby?"

"The same position you were in when you started it," replied the specialist.

"My God," exclaimed Lady Caroline, "do you mean I shall have to drive around Hyde Park in the Rolls for two hours with my feet hanging out of the window?"

A TASTE OF HONEY

Three daughters were all married on the same day, and that night their parents listened at the bedroom doors. They heard the first daughter laughing, the second crying and the third silent. The next morning their mother took them aside and asked them to explain.

"Well," said the first, "you always told me to laugh when something tickled me."

"Well," said the second, "you always told me to cry when something hurt me."

"Well," said the third, "you always told me not to speak when I had my mouth full."

VIVE LA DIFFERENCE 1

What's the difference between a circus and a high class whore house?
A circus is an array of cunning stunts.

VIVE LA DIFFERENCE 2

What's the difference between a donkey, an egg and sex?
You can beat a donkey, you can beat an egg, but you can't beat sex.

VIVE LA DIFFERENCE 3

What's the difference between a fat woman and an old maid?
The fat woman is trying to diet, the old maid is dying to try it.

THE SHORT CUT

HE : (pouring a drink) "Say when."
SHE : "After this drink."

THE PERFECT LOVER

A Frenchman with a nine inch tongue who can breath through his ears.

WILL POWER

She was complaining to the doctor that her husband was too old for her and couldn't consummate the marriage. The doctor gave her some pills for her husband and she left, promising him that she would let him know how things worked out. A week later, she came back and said, "Doctor, the pills were fine. For four days in a row, he did it morning and night."

"That certainly was an improvement," said the doctor.

She replied, "Oh yes! And just yesterday, he did it three times before he died."

FRICTION

A pretty young miss walked up to the bowlegged druggist and asked, "May I have some talcum powder, please."

He said, "Yes M'am, walk right this way."

She replied, "If I could walk that way, I wouldn't need any talcum powder."

ONE GOOD TURN...

Harry, a big powerful man, just didn't seem to hit it off with his fragile little wife after they got married. The house was filthy, the bed unmade, the dishes unwashed and her cooking was awful. After six months of this Harry made up his mind to kill her, using the huge weapon with which nature had endowed him. That night he made love to her for three hours. The next morning he staggered off to work, leaving his wife exhausted on the bed.

When he came home in the evening, he found the house spotlessly clean. Harry decided that the neighbours must have found the body and tidied up the house before the undertaker arrived. But in the kitchen he found his wife stark naked except for a little apron, preparing a six course dinner.

"But, darling..." he began.

"Say no more," she broke in, "you look after me properly, and I'll look after you."

His young wife had recently been displaying herself in various rather expensive new dresses, but he didn't want to ask her how she got the money out of their housekeeping allowance in case they had another row about how mean he was. But when his wife came in wearing a brand new silver mink jacket he was moved to ask her how she came by it.

"Oh, the most exciting thing dear, I won it in a raffle at the tennis club."

The next week he noticed that she was wearing a brand new pair of diamond earrings, and casually enquired how she came by them. The same answer :

"I won them in a raffle at the golf club." Then she went on : "Actually dear, I want to dash out again in a few minutes to get to another raffle reception—would you mind awfully running me a bath?"

"Well, my love," he replied, "I'm not sure that you ought to take a bath just now."

"Now why on earth not, dearest," she asked.

"Well darling I don't want you to get your raffle ticket wet."

FLUSHED OUT

A young English teacher was rather nervously giving her new class of eight year olds a grammar lesson. All was going well and she had explained the use of the word 'perhaps' to them without any interruptions.

"Now, Billy, will you make up a sentence to show that you understand how to use 'perhaps'?"

Billy stood up and after some thought said:

"If we are all very good perhaps teacher will let us go home early."

"Excellent," beamed the teacher, and, encouraged, turned to one of her more difficult pupils: "Now, I'm sure that you can give us another example, Jimmy."

Jimmy shambled sullenly to his feet and said: "Does it have to be made up, Miss?"

"No, it can be true, Jimmy, as long as the word 'perhaps' is used well."

Immediately, Jimmy started on his sentence: "When I saw Miss and the music teacher taking their pants off in the music room I thought perhaps they are going to shit in the piano."

STAND-IN

A big Yorkshire farmer found it necessary to go to London for several months and decided to leave one of his best workers in charge. "I want you to take care of things, Harry, as if I were here myself. Understand?" Harry nodded.

Four months later the boss farmer returned to find everything in shape. Said Harry, pointing things out, "the chicks have been laying plenty of eggs, the wheat has grown double strong, the vegetables are better than they've ever been, and as for those monthly spells your daughter used to have, I've even got those stopped."

YOU KNOW WHO...

The chorus girl was exuberant over receiving a role in a forthcoming play.

"I was made for the part!" she crowed happily.

"Shhh," cautioned her friend, "you don't have to tell everybody."

TURNING A TRICK

Manny Briggs thought that at last he had found a girl with an act that would put his theatrical agency on the map. He telephoned a big night club owner and launched into his selling line:

"No, but Al, I really have got one for you this time. She's stupendous, eighteen years old with long blonde hair, and . . . wow, Al, her figure is outa this world. Just get this: 66-22-36!"

The big night club owner was interested, and said he thought he could give the girl a dance routine right away: "What sort of a dance act does she have, Manny?"

"Well, she doesn't actually dance," came Manny's reply. "She just sorta crawls out there onto the stage and tries to stand up."

WHAM BAM

A zippy sports car had piled into a lamp post, and the driver sat swearing horribly at the safety belt which was still firmly holding him into his seat.

The local constable who arrived on the scene of the accident tried to calm the young man down by saying:

"Well sir, the safety belt did a lot for you. You ought to be thankful. If you hadn't been wearing it you would have gone straight through the windscreen like your lady."

"Good grief!" screamed the man. "You're joking! Just look what she's got in her hand."

THANK YOU MA'AM

A man is hit by a tennis ball two days before he is to be married. He is hurt in a vulnerable spot, so he goes to the doctor who says, "Sorry, old man, all I can do is put it in splints."

The wedding night, the bride takes off her dress, drops down her bra and says, "Look at these, aren't they beautiful? Virgin, never been touched by a human hand."

The bridegroom drops his pants and says, "Look at this, it hasn't even been uncrated."

SHEEPISH

A couple of farmers were walking back across the fields after a boozy lunch at the local when they spotted a lamb caught fast in a fence.

"Ahrr, Jem, I could wish that was Ursula Andress stuck in that fence like that," chortled one.

Jem replied: "Well, I'm just after wishing that it was dark."

A SHARP REJOINDER

A doctor performs an operation on a young woman. When she is ready to leave the hospital he tells her, "I've made a terrible mistake. I sewed the scissors up inside of you. However, it won't bother you. Go home and forget about it."

Two weeks later the young woman comes rushing into the doctor's office.

"Doctor, doctor," she cries, "you'll have to do something about those scissors. You must remove them at once. Two of my friends have been circumcised and a casual acquaintance has had his finger cut."

EXCOMMUNICATION

The husband wired home that he had been able to wind up his business trip a day early and would be home on Wednesday. When he walked into his apartment, however, he found his wife in bed with another man. Furious, he picked up his bag and stormed out; he met his mother-in-law on the street, told her what had happened and announced that he was filing suit for divorce in the morning.

"Give my daughter a chance to explain before you do anything," the older woman pleaded. Reluctantly, he agreed.

An hour later, his mother-in-law phoned the husband at his club.

"I knew my daughter would have an explanation," she said, a note of triumph in her voice. "She didn't receive your telegram!"

VIRGIN TERRITORY

He held her close against him, a warm glow of satisfaction covering them both.

"Am I the first man you've ever made love to?" he asked.

She studied him reflectively. "You might be," she said, "Your face looks very familiar."

RING MY CHIMES

The sweet seventeen year old girl had only been married for six weeks when her seventy-year-old husband died.

Talking about her brief marriage to her mother she said : "We were so terribly happy, and, mama, he was a wonderfully romantic lover. We used to make love all the time, and on Sunday mornings I remember he would make love to the rhythm of the church bells." She wept a little, and then went on : "I feel sure, mama, that if the fire engine hadn't dashed past clanging away on that last Sunday, he would still be alive now."

THE ACE OF HEARTS

A man was playing bridge with three women. He was bidding so badly that his partner was greatly annoyed.

After a few hours, he excused himself to go to the washroom. His partner exclaimed, "This is the first time all night that I know what he has in his hand."

VINTAGE '69

Did you hear about the French bridegroom who was so exhausted by the ceremony and the riotous wedding reception afterwards, that he fell asleep the minute his feet hit the pillow?

DEBUNKING

A honeymoon couple start off on a train. All they can get are two upper bunks opposite each other. During the night the bridegroom wakes up and calls to the bride, "Darling, come over into my bed."

"I can't," she answers. "I've no way of getting over."

"Look," says the bridegroom, "I have something long and hard. I'll turn it in your direction, use it to climb over."

"Oh, yes," came a voice from the lower bunk, "and how in hell do you think she'll get back?"

ALMS FOR THE POOR

A husband comes home and finds his wife in bed with a man. He is furious and wants to leave at once. The wife pleads, "Give me a moment to explain. This man came to my door an hour ago and asked for something to eat. I gave him a sandwich. I noticed that his shoes were worn out, so I looked in your closet and found a pair that you haven't had on your feet for five years, and I gave him the shoes to put on. Then I saw that his jacket was very torn, so I went back to your closet and found a jacket that you haven't worn for eight years. When he took his old jacket off to put yours on, I saw that his shirt was falling to pieces, so I opened your bureau drawer and gave him a shirt that you haven't worn for the past twelve years. Then as this man was going out of the door he turned to me and asked, "Is there anything else around here that your husband doesn't use?"

THE FAMILY WAY

They were crushed together in a passionate embrace when John decided that the psychological moment had arrived to tell Marsha.

"Darling," he murmured, "I think you're a marvellous person and I want you to know that I certainly appreciate your-ah-company, but as far as I'm concerned, marriage is for squares."

Marsha replied with a small sigh of pleasure.

"What I mean," John continued doggedly, "is you're more like a sister to me."

At that Marsha's eyes opened in surprise and she exclaimed, "Good Lord, what a home life you must have!"

MARITAL PROBLEM

". . . I'm in love with him, he loves me, we both enjoy the same things, he earns plenty of money, we're real happy together. . . . My problem is; what shall I tell my husband?"

THIS SPORTING LIFE

A married man, the father of three children, came to London. He met a beautiful girl. They spent the next five days together in a hotel room.

He then had to return to his home town, so he bid her a fond farewell.

As she said goodbye, she remarked, "I've been a good sport, haven't I? I haven't asked for a fur coat or diamond bracelet?"

Five months later she called him up at his factory in Manchester. He couldn't seem to place her. "This is the good sport," she reminded him. "I'm pregnant. I'm desperate. I'm going to have to commit suicide!" she wailed.

"You really are a Damned Good Sport," he commented.

A TASTY MORSEL

What is there in common between a passionate kiss and a spider?

Both lead to the undoing of the fly.

THE TRUANT

Every weekday for several months six commuters found that they invariably managed to travel in the same compartment. Breaking the ice one day, one of them suggested that they might pass the time with a few hands of poker. They started to introduce themselves: "My name's Hitchcock," beamed the man who had suggested the poker school. "I'm Hancock," announced the man on his right. And so it went round the compartment: "Alcock." "Woodcock." "Moorcock." Until they came to the last man, who shifted slightly and cleared his throat before muttering: "Vell, my name's Kuntz, an I don' think I better play with you boys."

ENGAGED

A woman walked into the ladies and saw a man standing up using the toilet.

Shocked, she exclaimed, "This is just for women!"

"So's this," he replied.

MAN'S BEST FRIEND

A rich American widow had for some years had a fantasy about finding a man who had never ever had any sexual experience with women.

The idea obsessed her completely, and she hired the services of an international detective agency who, after extensive and expensive investigations came up with a strapping young Australian who fitted the requirements. The negotiations were all completed, and the couple were married in New York.

On the wedding night the widow could hardly contain her excitement and she slipped her clothes off quickly in the bathroom and, clad in the flimsiest of negligees, drifted into the bedroom to greet her husband. She was absolutely flabbergasted to find that he had moved all the furniture, including the bed, onto the landing outside. "What on earth have you done with the furniture?" she shrieked in amazement.

"Well," drawled her husband, "I've never slept with a woman before, but I can tell you if it's anything like those there kangaroos, I'll need all the space I can get!"

THRICYCLE

The newlyweds were suffering from exhaustion and after an examination, their doctor advised, "It's not unusual for young people to overdo things during the first weeks of marriage. What you both need is rest. For the next month I want you to limit your sex to those days of the week with an 'r' in them. That is, Thursday, Friday Saturday."

Since the end of the week was approaching, the newlyweds had no immediate difficulty following the doctor's orders. But on the first night of scheduled rest the young bride found herself eager as a beaver. Hubby fell asleep, but she tossed and turned and finally nudged her spouse into partial wakefulness.

Expecting daylight, and confused with the darkness, he asked, "What day is it?"

"Mondray," said his bride, cuddling against him.

PSYCHO-THERAPY

The college psychology class was studying human reaction to sexual stimulus and of special interest was the frequency of amorous relations.

"How many students here," said the professor, "engage more than once a week?"

Five people raised their hands.

"And how many engage once a week?"

Ten hands went up.

"How many twice a month?"

Eight hands went up.

"Once a month?"

Four hands were raised.

"And how many once a year?"

A little guy in the back waved his hand frantically and giggled hysterically.

"If you engage only once a year," said the professor, "I don't see what you're so overjoyed about."

Flushed with excitement, the little guy said, "Yeah, but tonight's the night!"

PARLAY VOO . . .?

One evening, on an isolated part of the beach near Cannes, a beautiful young French girl tried to drown herself. Seeing this from a distance a man dashed down to the beach and into the water to try and save her. He was too late, but he brought her half naked body back to the beach and laid it on the sand while he went to call the police.

When he came back he was shocked to see another man making love to her, and he ran across the beach shouting: "Eh, monsieur, monsieur!" Out of breath, he reached the spot: "What are you doing, monsieur? That woman is dead!"

"Sacre bleu!!" shrieked the other man, leaping to his feet, "I thought she was an American."

FAIR EXCHANGE

Two couples go away on a two-week holiday together. After a week they are thoroughly bored. The men decide that if they exchange partners maybe life will take on new meaning. They all agree that it's an experiment worth trying. The morning after the exchange, one fellow says,

"I'm glad we tried this. It was exhilarating. Come on, let's go in the other room and see how the girls got on."

PHOTO FINISH

A young hippie bookseller was arrested by a member of the Vice Squad for peddling pornographic photographs.

"But you're making a big mistake," said the hippie. "These aren't dirty pictures!"

The officer selected a particularly intricate study of several naked men and women:

"Now you can't tell me that this isn't a dirty picture!"

"Aw, c'mon, man!" shrugged the hippie. "Haven't you ever seen five people in love before?"

THE EASY WAY IN

"How could you go to dinner with that wolf?" Alice asked her friend.

"Why not?" questioned the friend.

"Didn't you have trouble with him?" persisted Alice.

"No," her friend replied.

"How come?" Alice persevered.

"I said yes."

OVERTIME

"Oh I am so tired today," yawned a pretty young secretary to her girl friend. "Last night I couldn't go to sleep until after three."

"Well, goodness, no wonder you are tired," sympathised the friend. "Twice is usually quite enough for me!"

KISS AND MAKE UP

A man comes home very tired and despondent and tells his wife, "I was late for work today."

"I know," she says.

"I quarrelled with the boss," he adds.

"I know," she answers.

"He fired me," he says glumly.

"I know," she replies.

"How in the hell do you know?" he asks angrily.

"He told me," she replied.

"Screw the boss," said the irate husband.

"I did," said the wife. "You go back to work on Monday."

MAN ERRS

A smart London career girl had married a young farmer from Devon, and was far from pleased with his social manner. She determined to start improving him immediately and throughout the wedding reception she was continuously correcting his mistakes, telling him how to speak, which knife to use at table, and when to pass the salt. Finally the celebrations were all over, and they were in bed at last.

The flustered bridegroom fidgeted about between the sheets, unsure of himself and turning this way and that. Eventually half turning towards his new wife he stuttered:

"Could you pass the pussy, please?"

AIR CONDITIONED

A husband brings home a monkey and two rabbits to the one room in which he and his wife live. She looks dismayed. "What will they eat?"

"The same food as we do," says the husband.

"Where will they sleep?"

"At the foot of the bed."

"What about the smell?" she protests.

"They'll get used to it," he answered. "I did."

S.O.B. STORY

When an attractive young girl returned from her honeymoon she was in a state bordering on desperation, and decided to write to the "Aunt Marge" page of her weekly magazine:

"I am at my wit's end since it seems that the nice boy I married is really a sex-maniac. He never leaves me alone—he makes love to me all night without stopping, and then while I'm cooking breakfast, cleaning the house, while I'm in the bath, while I'm watching television, and so on. He just never stops! Can you please tell me what to do?

Signed,

'Exhausted'.

P.S.

Please excuse the jerky handwriting."

I'M SORRY, I'LL READ THAT AGAIN

Air-hostess: "Would you care for some of our TWA coffee?"
Male Passenger: "No, but I'd love some of your TWA Tea!"

BEASTLY APPETITES

A beautiful girl applied to the circus for a job as a lion tamer. "I already have a lion tamer," said the owner. "But I can take you on as an equestrian or as a trapeze artist."

"No," she protested, "I want to work as a lion tamer."

Just then the lion tamer walked in on them with blood oozing from his arm. "A lion mauled me," he moaned. "I won't go on tonight."

"Okay," said the owner to the girl, "the job is yours." The girl entered the lions' cage, took off her shoes and her stockings, then her dress, her bra and her petticoat. She folded her apparel neatly. Then, naked, she lay down on the floor of the cage using her clothes as a pillow.

Two lions walked over to her and started licking her face, her neck, her breasts.

The owner turned to his lion tamer still nursing his wounded arm and asked, "Why can't you do that?"

"I can," the man answered, "if you'll just remove the lions."

A CLOSE SHAVE

A man is in a barber's shop getting a shave and a manicure. He says to the manicurist, "How about going out to dinner with me tonight?"

"I can't," she answers, "I'm married."

"Tell your husband," says the customer, "that you have to work tonight."

"You tell him," says the manicurist. "He's shaving you!"

IDENTIKIT

Three men were in court before the judge on various charges. Asked to state their occupations, one said he was a cork soaker, the second man said that he was a coke sacker, and the third man said that he was the real thing.

MEASURE FOR MEASURE

A man is sitting in his living room reading the newspaper when his wife comes over and slaps him.

"What was that for?' asks the indignant husband.

"That's for being a lousy lover."

A little while later, the husband goes over to where the wife is sitting watching TV and he gives her a resounding smack.

"What was that for?" she yells at him.

To which he answers, "For knowing the difference."

SAVOIR FAIRE

Two Frenchmen are standing on the platform of the train that is pulling out of Paris. One of them waves to a friend at the station and calls :

"Thanks loads; had a marvellous time; your wife was a wonderful lay!" Then he turns to the man standing next to him and says, "It's not true. She's no good at all. I just wanted the husband to feel good."

TRAFFIC JAM

A Frenchman and his girl were driving past the outskirts of Paris when the man stopped his car and persuaded his girl to climb under the car with him where he could make love to her.

Half an hour later, a gendarme tapped him on the feet and asked him what he was doing.

"Repairing my car," replied the Frenchman.

"Monsieur," replied the policeman, "I'm afraid I cannot accept your explanation. Do you know that behind you is a long line of cars? You are holding up the President of France, the Commissioner of Paris, and the Abbey of Notre Dame—and furthermore Monsieur, someone has stolen your car."

OVER OPTIMISTIC

The professor asked a girl in his physiology class, "What part of the body expands to ten times its natural size under an emotional impact?"

Blushing, the girl said, "I'd rather not answer that."

The professor called on the boy sitting next to her, who promptly replied, "The pupil of the eye."

The professor turned back to the girl and said, "Your confusion shows: one, that you didn't study your lesson; two, that you have a dirty mind; and three, that you will be sadly disappointed."

HOLY WATER

Over drinks, one man asks another, "Ever see an ice cube with a hole in it?"

The other responds, "Yes, I was married to one for twenty years."

STALE MATE

A couple, who were married for years, were making love. He asked, "Dear, am I hurting you?"

"No," she replied, "but why do you ask?"

"You moved," he replied.

EAGER TO PLEASE

A boy meets a girl at a discotheque and she asks him to take her back to her flat. After a lot of kissing the girl refuses to let him make it with her, telling him :

"Look, boyo, anybody that makes me has to have two things—a brand new sports car and a cock at least twelve inches long."

The boy said he would be back, and left it at that.

Two days later he drew up outside her flat in a brand new Aston Martin. The girl gasped in disbelief, but he went on :

"As for that other thing, well my doctor says he can cut it down to any size you like."

COCKSURE

At four o'clock one morning the Madame was most surprised to hear the doorbell ring long and loud. Yawning, she opened the door and stared tiredly at a man who had both arms and both legs in plaster.

"I want a woman," he stated.

"Oh, why don't you go home and go to sleep instead : my girls have all turned in for the night anyway."

"Look, lady, when I say I want a woman, I mean I want a woman and now !"

The Madame began to get cross : "Well, let's be realistic. What on earth do you think you could do with a woman in your condition ?"

"Listen, lady," replied the man, "I rang the bell, didn't I?"

THROUGH A GLASS DARKLY

The housemaster found two of his school-boys masturbating and reprimanded :

"If you keep that up you will go blind !"

Only slightly abashed the two boys glanced at each other and the first boy said to the second :

"Well, let's just do it until we need glasses."

A travelling salesman was just on the point of checking into a hotel when he caught sight of a stunning piece of skirt who was without doubt giving him the full 'come-hither' treatment. He strolled over to her, and nonchalantly exchanged a few words with her, behaving as though he had known her all his life. Then they both walked back to the reception desk and booked in as man and wife.

After a one-night stay, the salesman went to collect his bill and check out. He was appalled to be presented with a bill for £100.

"Look here, this is out of the question. I've only been here one day!"

"Yes, sir," replied the receptionist, "but your wife has been here a month."

DISCOUNTING SHEEP

A ventriloquist, driving across country from one engagement to another, put up for the night at a farm miles off the beaten track. In the morning he amazed the farmhands by practising his voice-throwing in the farm yard and, apparently, making various animals talk.

One of the yokels grabbed his arm and asked: "Here, can youse make all them animals talk?"

"Why, of course," replied the ventriloquist.

"Ar, well," muttered the yokel, drawing him to one side and lowering his voice, "if that there sheep on the end there says anythin' about me, I tell 'ee now it's all a dirty lie!"

SOUL MATES

A man presented his wife with a tombstone while she was still living. On it he had had carved, "Here lies my wife, cold as usual."

The wife went out and bought her husband a tombstone. She presented it to him with the inscription: "Here lies my husband, stiff at last."

FOREIGN PARTS

A French woman dies. At the funeral the husband is calm and composed, but the lover is beside himself with anguish. He throws himself on the coffin, moaning and groaning. Finally the husband goes over to him and says, "Console yourself; I plan to marry again."

SILLY QUESTION

A man asked a prostitute, "What's your ceiling price?"

She answered, "Same as on the floor."

PUSSY CAT

A pert and rather debbie young actress, just out of drama school, was chatting loudly at a theatre party: "I must say that I'm twenty-eight years old and I still have my cherry."

The leading lady, who certainly didn't have hers and hadn't had it for years, purred at the prissy little angel, "So, you still have your cherry, do you? Fascinating, do tell me just one thing . . . does it get in your way when you screw?"

SELLERS MARKET

A man goes on a business trip to buy up some metal. He is to be gone a week. After the week he wires his wife: "Busy, still buying."

Each week for three or four more weeks he sends his wife the same wire.

At the end of six weeks she telegraphs to him: "Come home at once, darling, before I start selling what I think you're buying."

There was a young man of Kildare
Who was having a girl in a chair.
    At the sixtieth stroke
    The bloody thing broke
And his rifle went off in the air.

There was a young man of Cape Horn
Who wished he had never been born.
    And he wouldn't have been
    If his father had seen
That the tip of the rubber was torn.

There was a young student of John's,
Who was keen to bugger the swans.
    Said the faithful hall-porter:
    "Pray take my daughter,
But the birds are reserved for the dons!"

The typists at Wheesly and Beasly
All fornicate steadily and easily.
    In this pleasant way
    They add to their pay,
Which at Wheesly and Beasly is measley.

There was an old girl from Kilkenny
Whose usual charge was a penny.
    For half of that sum
    You could roger her bum
—A source of amusement to many.

That naughty old lady of Greece
Said : "What I prefer to a piece
    Is to have my pudenda
    Rubbed hard by the enda
The little pink nose of my niece."

OVERREACHED HIMSELF

Three suitors called on a girl, and they had to sleep together in the spare bed. Mother and daughter listened outside the door to their conversation.

The first was heard to say that his aunt might leave him ten thousand pounds.

"That's the man for you," says mother.

The next was heard to say that his father was just going to make him a director in the family firm.

"No, that's the man for you," says mother.

The third man was heard to say: "Bill you're lying on the end of my cock, move off it, will you?"

"No, I am not lying on it," said Bill.

"Then it's lying on top of you, and Jack is on the end of it!"

"That's the man for me," said the daughter.

IN A FLAP

Two young girls who were close friends used to exchange confidences.

One day, Mary said : "I've got some smashing news Jane, listen to this, I'm getting engaged to a chap who has promised me a Rolls Royce for a wedding present, and then he's going to give me a Fashion Shop to run, after we're married."

"Congratulations, darling," said the other, a little bleakly.

The next time they met, Jane said :

"Oh, by the way Mary, I'm putting the Banns up for me and a chap at the office."

"Has he any money?" enquired her friend.

"No, I must confess, but he says his phallus is so long that six pigeons can perch on it at once. You must admit that would help a marriage to go."

* * *

Several months later they met again. "How's the Rolls Royce?" said Jane.

"Listen, dear, we were always truthful with each other, I'll admit it, the Rolls turned out to be a Ford Popular, and the Fashion House turned out to be assisting in a little tobacconists run by his father."

"Mine was a terrible disappointment, too," said the other girl. "The honest truth is, that only four pigeons can perch on it, and even then the end one has to keep flapping."

TO(I)LET

A Rent Collector got a job in the Black Country. His Chief told him :

"It's different here, the houses are rough, the people are rough, you've got to be persistent." Armed with this information the Collector made his first call—a small boy answered the door :

"Is your mother in?"

"No, she went out when me dad came in."

"Fetch your dad then, will you?"

"Can't, he went out when me brother came in."

"Where is your brother then?"

"He cleared off when me big sister came in."

"Can your sister give me the rent?"

"No, she went out when I came in."

"Look here son, someone's got to pay—No rent, no house, see? You'll all be turned out of this place, see?"

"But look here, mister, this isn't the house, it's the W.C."

FACTS OF LIFE

Johnny came home from school and said : "Oh we had a very extra special film at school this afternoon." "Did you?" said dad.

"Yes," said Johnny, "and all the girls were sent out of the room."

Pa looked at Ma, and changed the subject. When Johnny had gone, Pa looked at Ma again, and she said : "Well, you've got to discuss it with him sometime, even if he is only ten."

Just before bed, father said : "Er, hum, er, Johnny, I want to have a little talk with you. What was that film about, the one where the girls were sent outside?"

"Football," said Johnny.

OLD CHINESE CUSTOM?

A lady Professor was lecturing the Women's Institute. "Do you know," she said, "that somewhere in the world a woman is giving birth to a child every minute of the day and night— What are we going to do about it?"

"I know," said an old countrywoman, "find her, and stop her at it."

I COVER THE WATERFRONT

Or : *It's the knack as does it!*

I really love the BLACK COUNTRY, I come from Wolverhampton
But BUSHEY PARK I did prefer, and there took out my HAMPTON
I said : Sweet girl just be a pearl, give me your TAPLOW do
She said : You may enjoy a lay, if you lay MARLOW too.

I found the way to EGHAM on, to TICKLEHAM and fookham,
And when I sought to BURNHAM up, by gad I'd really COOKHAM !
Now, listen Gents, to these events, you don't get sex for gins, or
Gifts of chocs, or frocks, or clocks, it is the knack as WINDSOR

I said : My Queen, here's COCKPOLE GREEN, with that she was most smitten;
Please don't be SLOUGH, but quickly go, oh how I have LONG DITTON
My HAMPTON COURT, but stopped at naught, and broke, in spite of pains,
Her MAIDENHEAD, and left the bed a lovely view of STAINES

*SPLITTING THE DIFFERENCE

Mary had a little blouse, twas busted all to bits,
And everywhere that Mary went, it showed her little tits.
Mary had a little skirt, twas split right down the front,
And everywhere that Mary went, she had to sit down all the time

*BAWDY GEORDIE

There was a young man of Newcastle
Who did a peculiar trick,
He opened the vent of his astle
And deftly inserted his wick

He didn't do this for honour
He didn't do this for pelf,
He did it to please an old comrade
Who'd told him to roger himself

An oversexed lady named Bright
Insists on two dozen a night.
A fellow named Chedder
Had the brashness to wed her—
His chance of survival is slight.

SHOOTING PRACTICE

A captain of artillery, a sergeant and a bombardier were arguing about the act of love. The captain declared it was ninety percent pleasure and ten percent work; the sergeant said it was ten percent pleasure and ninety percent work. The bombardier, who was scared of both, said it was fifty percent work, fifty percent pleasure.

They decided to ask the first person who came along, and it happened to be a humble gunner. In answer to the question, he said:

"Of course it's a hundred percent pleasure. If it wasn't you lot would make us gunners do it for you."

GEORGE AND THE DRAGON?

A man in a country hotel, a commercial traveller, rang down to the reception desk and said: "Send up a nice whore." The proprietor's wife was very angry, and told her husband to go up and throw the man out. He refused, because he didn't want to lose a good customer, and he said the request was natural and harmless.

The wife said. "If you won't, I will," and off she went upstairs.

There was a fearful racket for about twenty minutes, after which the traveller came down and said: "I suppose that's all you can get in country towns, but she was a tough old bitch. I damn near had to rape her."

STRETCHING IT A BIT

A woman complained to the doctor that her breasts hurt her. He asked a few questions, and she said she was sure it was because her husband would insist on an unnatural practice.

"What sort of unnatural practice?"

"Well, doctor, he will insist on sleeping with my nipple in his mouth!"

"Nothing unusual in that madam," says the medico.

"What, when we're sleeping in separate beds!"

WHORE YOU KIDDIN'?

It was during the war that a Polish officer who did not fully understand the language, picked up a high class prostitute in London, and was taken to her flat. After a remarkable supper with wine, she took him to bed for a series of repeat performances.

After a very good breakfast she helped him into his overcoat, handed him his hat, and said: "What about some money?"

"Oh, but Madame, a Polish officer and a gentleman could never accept money from a woman, it would be a dishonour."

A country chap went up to London during the war, and he could not find a lodging. He by chance met a village maiden who had gone up to town some years before to look for work, and who remembered him.

Rationing was very strict, and the man was very pleased to get a big meal, with food unlimited.

"Go on" she said, "eat, I'm well in with the grocer. Have some wine, I'm well in with the vintner. Have a cigar, I'm well in with the tobacconist."

The visitor was overwhelmed. He rose to make up the fire. "Put plenty on" she said, "I'm well in with the coal-man."

Then she tucked up to the blaze, pulled her skirts well up to warm her thighs, and the young man said: "Mary, be careful!"

"Be careful—why?"

"I should hate you to burn your ration book."

BY THEIR WORDS SHALL YE KNOW THEM

During the war a German spy was dropped behind the British lines with orders to report on what regiments were moving up to the front. The spy sent back such perfect reports that he was afterwards taken before General Rommell to receive the Iron Cross.

"Tell me, Feldwebel Shmit," said the General, "what is the secret of your success?"

The spy explained that he had concealed himself by a Sewage Works, and as the first regiment marched past he heard:

"I thay, Thecil old darling, do you notith a dweadful pongo?"

"Yeth Basil, ithent it fwiteful?" so he knew that must be the Artists Rifles. As the next lot came past he heard: "Jock, d'ye reckon we could dree oot some o' yon stuff, an' smoke it in oor wee pipes" so that must be the Aberdeen Light Infantry.

Finally, he heard men saying: "By cripes Jack, can you smell a mucking smell of mucking grit that stinks like a navvy's piss-corner?"

These, Mein Herr, could only be the South Staffords.

SWEET AND LOW

The old Squire had an estate, and during the war he woke up one morning to find the Americans camped all over it. Honour demanded that he ask the Colonel to dine.

After dinner the dignified old family butler said:

"How do you like your coffee Sir?"

The Colonel was rather an abrupt man, lost in these surroundings, and he replied:

"Lissen, Ah likes ma corfee like Ah likes ma wimmen—hot and sweet, d'you gerrit?"

"Yes Sir," said the butler, unflappable, "black, or white Sir?"

Belle de l'Amour was the most beautiful and exotic courtesan in France under the Empire. When the king had finished with her she set up shop in a fashionable boulevard, and charged one thousand francs a night.

The Cadets of Saint Cyr had heard many stories of her voluptuous charms and passionate nature, and the conversations in the barrack rooms often ended on the note of what any one of them would do if he won the national lottery.

"Lottery!" cried a bright recruit, "that gives me an idea." It was there and then agreed among them that every Cadet should pay one franc, and as there were a thousand of them that would just be the courtesan's fee. Then they would hold a raffle, and the lucky winner should spend a night with the lady.

Thus it was that young Du Pont, the son of a noble house, appeared before the lady. When she saw a boy of 19 she went to send him away, but when she saw the thousand francs, she changed her mind.

The following morning, pulling a transparent silk slip over her voluptuous body, she sat up and asked how such a youth came by so much money, and he told her the whole story.

Her romantic French heart was deeply moved: "Ah, mon petit cheri, quel sentiment!" she cried, and said in the circumstances she felt she ought to give him his money back. The idea thrilled the youth, and as he departed he kissed her and held out his hand. She reached for her jewelled purse and—gave him a franc.

LOCKSMITH LAUGHS AT LOVE

A certain firm set on a commercial traveller. His only qualification was that he was the son of a Director, and had failed at several other jobs. They sent him out after a good "spec" and told him to report next day.

Next day he came in looking very washed up, and without the order. He explained that while driving across the New Forest his car broke down, and when he knocked on a cottage door to ask for help, the place was occupied by a young widow, who asked him to stay the night.

"Go on, go on," said the Sales Manager . . . "and you spent the night screwing? I didn't think you'd got that much sense!"

"You bet I did!" said the young man, "You see, when we went to bed she told me the lock on her bedroom door was broken."

"I see, and you didn't get much sleep?"

"That's what I keep trying to tell you, I felt in honour bound to try and mend it, and it took longer than I thought."

YES SIR, THAT'S MY BABY

A traveller was crossing a wild and lonely moor late at night when his car broke down, and he walked to an isolated farm for help. The farmer had no phone, and anyway it was late and a rough night, so the farmer offered a bed.

"You can either share a single bed with the baby," he said, "or kip down on the hay in the barn."

The traveller thought he wouldn't want to be wet on by any babies, so he chose the barn, and had a pretty rotten night of it.

In the morning he awoke to see a big-breasted rosy-cheeked girl of sixteen entering with a pail: "Who are you?" he said.

"I'm the baby of the family, who are you?"

"I'm the stupid prat that chose to sleep in the barn."

ON THE CARPET

A man was up in London for a Conservative conference, and having a free day was exploring the streets when he got lost.

After a time he suffered an urgent need to ease his bowels, and nowhere could he see. The situation was desperate, so he stopped a stranger and explained the difficulty. The stranger said: "I see from your badge you are a Tory, follow me, it's not far." With which he took him around a few quick corners, entered a Georgian portal, and took him down a long carpeted passage.

"Are you sure this is all right?"

"Quite all right, old boy, just follow."

Thus they went through a gilded lobby into a vast room lit with candelabra, and hung with old masters.

"Here."

"What here, on this posh carpet?"

"Yes, here, on this posh carpet."

The man felt very much better. "Where now?" he said.

"The next," said his new friend, "is to run the hundred yards in eleven seconds, you're in the Russian Embassy."

ONE AND ONE MAKE THREE

A boy of 12 went to his father with a little girl of 10, a neighbour's daughter.

"Dad," he said, "we want to get married."

"Yes, son, in ten years."

"No dad, now!"

"What are you going to live on?"

"We can manage on her pocket money and mine."

Said father (playing the joke along): "Oh, I see, and what if she has a baby?"

"Well dad, nothing's happened so far."

CALF LOVE

There was a young man went to the doctor and said he wanted to get married but he was worried about the small size of his member. The doctor advised him to go and stay on a farm, dip his wick in milk several times a day, and have it sucked by a calf.

Some months later when they met in the street, the doctor said:

"How's your marriage?"

"Oh, I didn't get married doctor, I bought a calf instead."

BITCH IN SHEEP'S CLOTHING

It was way out in the wild west, and women were very scarce. The tenderfoot went into the saloon, and asked the barman where he could go to get sex. The barman said: "Back o' Jake's place down the track, there's a nice young sheep in a barn. Give Jake a dollar, and you're fixed."

When the tenderfoot arrived at the barn he found a nice young sheep, very clean and decked with ribbons. But Jake came out and told him to clear off. "Listen, Jake, I got my dollar."

"Listen, I said scram t'hell outa it. Sheriff's keepin' her now."

WOOL OVER HIS EYES

The African Chief was very suspicious. His youngest and curviest wife had given birth to a near-white child. He pointedly called the Missionary's attention to it, and at the same time fondled his spear in a thoughtful manner.

The Missionary was calm: "Listen, O chief," he said, "look at all those sheep over there on the mountain (the Chief looked), well, one of those white sheep has just had a black lamb."

"Fair enough, O man of God, you no tell, me no tell."

SWEET CONVERSATION

A woman went into a chemist's shop and said: "Do you fit ladies with dutch caps?" "Certainly madam, certainly," beamed the chemist.

"Well go and wash your dirty filthy hands and serve me with a quarter of cough drops."

BIRDS OF A FEATHER

There was a certain respectable suburb in which there was a high class brothel, which had everything, even a high class parrot. When the Madam had made her pile, and the girls were going off a bit, she decided to sell up. On the day of the sale most of the local worthies were present, bidding for luxury carpets, curtains, etc.

When the parrot was auctioned the auctioneer called: "What am I bid for this beautiful bird . . . five pounds . . . six pounds . . . seven pounds ten." There was a silence, and the parrot shouted out: "Aw, come on daddy, don't be a mean scrooge, make it ten and I'll give you a gam as well."

The bird was finally bought by the Mayor, but he was a bit wary of it, and kept it covered up with a cloth whenever there was an official reception. One day the Mayor was receiving a religious convention when the Bishop's wife, overcome by curiosity, pulled the cloth from the cage. The parrot shouted:

"Oh, hallo! New house, new girls, new lighting, same old customers, howdy Charlie!"

ACTING THE GOAT

A city visitor drove up to a farm, just as the farmer's son was walking up the road wearing wellington boots. It was a fine hot summer day, so the stranger enquired: "Why are you wearing gumboots on a day like this?"

"I allus wears these when I goes courting," replied the yokel.

The visitor could not see why gumboots were essential for courting, so the young man explains: "You've got to have some way of keeping that nanny-goat's back legs still."

MADE A COCK-UP OF IT

There was a poultry farmer who was having no luck at all. His birds just refused to lay or breed. He was telling his troubles one day in a pub to another poultry farmer . . .

"You've come to the right man," said the other, "I've got the randiest cockerel in the business. He's wearing my birds out, you can have him for a quid. If he doesn't liven up every bird you've got, you can have your money back."

The man took the bird home, and really he had a devilish look in his eye. When he was let loose the next morning he not only covered all the pullets within the hour, but he'd done his stuff with a large flock of ducks as well.

After lunch every goose in the place was heard squawking, and by teatime even the turkey-hens were looking placid, and had begun to lay. When the new owner went out in the evening to give the bird a splendid meal, he couldn't find him. He looked everywhere, and at last, peering over a bank, he saw his cockerel stiff and motionless on his back, his legs in the air.

The poultry farmer was broken-hearted . . . the bird had worked himself to death . . . what a tragedy. "Never mind, old son," he said, as he approached, "you had a lovely death, and I'll never eat you, but give you a decent funeral."

"Go away you bloody stupid fool," hissed the cock, "I'm trying to fox down that damn vulture hovering up there."

RETORT COURTEOUS

There was a really curvy girl at a dance, and all the smart men were after her. A spotty youth was much attracted, but he couldn't get a look in. However, during a "Gentleman's Excuse-me" he rushed up and grabbed her.

"Go away!" she glared, "I'm not going to dance with a child."

"Oh, sorry Miss, I didn't know you were pregnant."

HAD HIM TAPED!

A spinster of 40 had a brother at sea, and he sent her a pair of parrots in a double cage. The spinster was intrigued to know which was the cock and which was the hen, as they were exactly alike, so she consulted a Vet.

"Watch them," said the vet, "the one that gets on top is the male."

"I DO watch them," said the lady, "but they never do anything!"

"Then creep down at dawn and have a peep, and when you know which is the cock, be sure and mark it."

The spinster obeyed instructions, and caught the birds in the very act of mating. Thrilled to bits, she tied a white tape round the cock's neck.

The following Sunday the Vicar came to tea. As he removed his coat the cock parrot shouted:

"Hallo, so you've been caught doing a woman as well, have you?"

SAGA OF PASSION

There was a spinster schoolteacher who was plain, skinny and with an impediment in her speech.

She longed for a man, and used to comfort herself by reading 'respectable' erotic stories, namely the adventures of the great classical gods. This only made her worse, but one night a strange thing happened . . . she dreamed that a big blond naked man came to her bed, ripped off her long nightgown, and raped her again and again.

In the morning as he was about to depart through the window, she begged him to stay.

"I must return to Valhalla," he said, "I'm Thor."

"Tho am I, but wathenth it marvellouth!"

STANDING OVATION

There was an elderly Peer who woke up one morning and rang for his valet: "Jenkins, I find I have an erection."

"Congratulations, Sir!—shall I fetch Her Ladyship."

"Certainly not! Fetch the car, this is a West End job!"

ANSWER TO A MAIDEN'S PRAYER

There was a spinster who had a parrot, and it swore and used some terrible expressions. When the Vicar called she covered it up for shame, and the Vicar enquired the reason.

"I couldn't repeat it," she said, but the Vicar pulled the cover off, and that wicked bird let out a mouthful.

"I'll have to have his neck pulled, the villain," said the spinster.

"Certainly not, Miss Tavvinitt," he said, "I have a lady parrot, a parrot of the utmost virtue, who prays by day and night. I'm sure that if we put them together she will reform him."

This was agreed upon, and the following day Miss Tavvinitt took her bird round to the Vicarage, and he was put in the cage with the devout lady parrot.

Immediately he misbehaved, shouting: "Lift your tail up, come on, I want sex, what are we waiting for!"

Before the Vicar and the spinster could do a thing about it, the lady parrot replied: "What the bloody hell d'you think I've been praying for all these years?"

OLD AGE CREEPING ON

There was a blooming young girl who asked her old grannie how often married people had sex. Grannie explained, it wasn't as simple as that.

Newly married people might have it every night, people in their thirties, three times a week. In the forties and fifties, it might slow up to once a week.

"But grannie, what about people over say, 65?"

"Well then I reckon it's once a quarter."

"Grannie, you're 75, and grandad's 85, how often . . ."

"Once a year," croaked the old dame . . . "Heh, heh . . . TONIGHT ! !"

TWISTED PERSONALITY

Here lies the body of poor old Mick
Who went through life with a corkscrew wick
He spent his days on a fruitless whim
To find a girl with a corkscrew quim.
He found one at last, but fell down dead,
When he found it had a left-hand thread.

WRINGING WET

It was a hard-fought rugger match, and the lads staggered to an inn for some throat oil. After a few pints two players, they were opponents and strangers, went round the back to pump ship. Suddenly one burst out laughing, and said :

"Pardon me old chap, but ho ho ! your John Thomas—I hope I'm not being rude—is all twisted. Did you get mangled in the scrum or sumpin ?"

"No old feller," replied the other, "it's always been corkscrew-shape, I must admit it bothers me a bit."

"Tell you what," said the first, "my Guvnor's a doctor, come round on Monday, I'll get the old man to have a look at it for you."

Monday came, and the young man kept the appointment. His new friend was waiting, and said :

"Howdyer get on old chap ?"

"Oh, it's nothing that plastic surgery won't put right."

"Yes, but how did it get like that ?"

"That was through my mother being a widow, and prudish as well."

"I'm not with you old boy, elaborate a little."

"Well, your father has just explained to me for the first time, that when you have a pee, you shake it, you don't wring it out."

LIMERICKS X

A plump stewardess named Byote
Took too many rolls when afloat,
Said her Ma : Tons of grub
Couldn't fill out *that* tub,
You've been messing about in a boat!

She was reared in a bleak institution
And grew up in great destitution,
She married, the bitch,
A man old and rich
And always condemns prostitution

There were three young maidens of Twickenham
Who wanted Tom, Harry, and Dick in 'em,
They prayed hard to Venus
Saying : Surely, between us,
We can lengthen, and strengthen, and thicken 'em

The foxhunting Countess of Mourne
Was hunting her spouse in the corn,
By God did she swear
When she saw the Au Pair
Go to ground as he flourished his horn

Said a Printing House man to his bird :
To wait for the Chapel's absurd
And tho' it would fret 'er
He'd slip in a letter
And act out a four-letter word

THE MODEST MINI MAIDEN

Tune: The Red Flag (Tannenbaum)

Some pad their chests and dye their curls
That's just to nark the other girls,
And tho' they are like walking-sticks
I show my legs to get my kicks

Chorus

> Then raise the mini skirts on high
> And bare another piece of thigh
> Tho' young men pinch and old men leer
> I'll keep my hemline right up here!

My mother says I'm in disgrace
Disclosing pants all edged with lace,
I'll leave them off, what do I care
If only MEN will stop and stare

Chorus

> Then raise the mini skirts on high, etc.

And now, dear girls, advice to you,
When men do what you drove them to,
You call a policeman on the spot,
To deal with such a dirty lot

Chorus

> Then raise the mini skirts on high, etc.

For you can raise your skirts on high
Yet pose a virgin modesty,
Stoke up the fire, but never quench
Until he's firmly hooked, my wench.

Chorus

> Then raise the mini skirts on high
> And show another piece of thigh
> Tho' young men pinch and old men leer
> I'll keep my hemline right up here!

BY THEIR FRUITS SHALL YE KNOW THEM

When reading the wafflings of great men of old
Eve fell for the serpent, or so we are told
She must have this reptile so long strong and firm
That even the thought of it caused her to squirm.
But Adam had got it! The problem to grapple—
When would he uncoil it? "She offered an *apple*"
And thus there began the erroneous libel—
No *apple* is mentioned in anyone's bible

As everyone knows, without going to College,
She gave him *the fruit of the banned Tree of Knowledge*
And the fruit Eve thrust forth with lascivious zest
The vulgar call *tit* and the learned call *breast*
So that's why the Savants in High Schools and Halls
(Who say *nuts* or else *taters* when speaking of balls)
Have classified breasts, and the way women show them
In various grades: *By their fruits shall ye know them!*

Some girls have nothing but two little puce-berries
In size and appearance like rather small *gooseberries*,
And others again, without sexy shapes
Can present to their sweethearts mere *cherries* or *grapes*
There's small hope of marriage for those would-be Mums
Who've nothing to offer but *lemons* or *plums*
The fruits that men fall for are bulgy and swell-uns
Like *coconuts, grape-fruit,* or well-rounded *melons*

Girls hardly get any man's serpent to rise
Unless they are blessed with a bust of good size,
But don't overdo it. They only get bumpkins
Whose bra's are just sackfuls of bloody great *pumpkins.*
Last : Ladies ! Take comfort if your tits are small
Far better have small ones than no bust at all,
Grown women I've seen—on their chests not a thing !
Save two tiny spots where a bee left a sting

* CHEESED OFF

Under the spreading chestnut bough
There sat a young milk-maid, a-milking a cow
Along came the farmer, and gave her the sack,
So she turned the cow over, and poured the milk back

* ROMANTIC LOVE

The love of a beautiful maiden
The love of a strong young man
The love of romantic sweethearts
Existed since time began.
But the greatest love of all loves
Greater than that of a mother,
Is the tender, delicate, intimate—lust
Of one randy sod for another!

* THE EXCEPTION

With vain regret I oft remember
Those happy days of youth and fun
When all my limbs were soft and tender
Did I say all? Well, all but one.
Gone are those happy days for ever
Those halycon days of lust and fun,
Now, all my joints, and limbs, are stiffer
Did I say all? Well, all but one.

BOSOM FRIENDS?

When I look at Janet and Jessie and Julia
It seems Nature's plan is very peculia
For some girls are carrying more than a plenitude
While others are moaning they-haven't-got-any-tude.

Thus girls with full hip lines and very good legs
Are filled full of envy by two skinny pegs,
And lassies whose sweaters are tenanted houses
Stare jealous of others with loose flapping blouses

In other men's pastures the grass is much greener
Say Aggie the Scraggy and plump Wilhelmina.

* DOUBLE COVER

When the Censor saw the Dancer
He became a flaming red
First he stuttered, then he stammered
Then he caught his breath and said :

"I am shocked beyond description
At the length to which you've gone
I can't allow this exhibition
Twice as much, you must put on."

When the Dancer heard the Censor
She was very quick to heed
To her dressing-room she hastened
And put on another bead !

* OLD FIDDLES, BEST TUNES

I told my friend one Summer's day
My husband's safe and will not stray
I'll not believe a tale that's told,
He's decent, fine, — and very old

* * *

My dear ! How true it is to say
He strayed with me the other day !
Old fiddles play the very best
And play as often as the rest !

LOVELY ENGLISH MAIDEN

See that beauty standing there
Bootblack eyes and Woolworth's hair,
Plastic coat and kinky boots
Blonde (but very dark at roots)
Moth gashed big and quim gashed bigger
All she lacks is face and figure

* * *

Those tatty nylons full of holes
Those tatty shoes with cardboard soles
Those skinny legs : a skirt on high
Betrays a piece of skinny thigh,
Skinny bottom, skinny mind,
Behold, this piece of womankind—
This Work of God, this painted face,
Behold ! the Mother of the Race.

* TIME OFF IN LOO?

We see it every morning, it happens every day
A double file of female staff meanders on its way,
The thing that puzzles all the men, and gives the boss grey hairs
Is why, when serving Nature's calls, they have to go in PAIRS?
Perhaps the trip's demanding, and the toilet dark and lonely?
But two by two they reach the loo by the door marked Ladies Only.

The poor Boss stands, and tears his hair, he's simply mad with grief,
The day's production goes to pot, while girls go on relief,
At two o'clock each afternoon, the match begins once more,
But what on earth goes on all day, behind that toilet door?
The only way that I can see to make production boom,
Is to move the whole damn Typing Pool inside the Ladies Room!

*OVER THE HILL

It's not the grey hair that makes a man old
Or the faraway look in his eye, so I'm told :
But when the mind seeks a contract the body can't fill,
You're over the hill brother, over the hill.

You can fool the dear wife with the cleverest lies,
You can tell her the tale and pull wool on her eyes,
But when she wants an encore, and you say you're ill,
You're over the hill brother, over the hill

When you gaze on a stripper, and just heave a sigh
When you hear a bum joke, and you laugh till you cry,
When sex is plain duty, and never a thrill
You're over the hill brother, over the hill

Love is a conflict the battle is keen,
There are so many rounds in the old magazine
When you've fired your last shell and you cannot refill
You're over the hill brother, over the hill

Repair the old howitzer, boy, if you can,
But oyster and eggs cannot make you a man,
No vigour can last got from powder or pill,
You're over the hill brother, over the hill

This is my story, alas and alack,
When you've squeezed out the toothpaste you can't put it back,
If "Whoopee" you're needing, well don't wait until
You're over the hill brother, over the hill

An Optician's clerk named Mollasses
Had a wick far too small for the lassies,
Much pleasure he'd missed
Till his boss made a list
Of spinsters who needed thick glasses

A Pools-winning woman of Fife
Said : Marriage is nothing but strife,
(Her husband asked : Gwen
Do we enter again?)
With my draws up?—Why not on your life!

A Canon of very high station
Wed a woman of no reputation
They'd a child in ten weeks
And whenever she speaks,
It's only to knock fornication

A French woman Maquis named Blérot
Who took Winston C. for her hero
Said : He told the *Entente*
It was hard, tough and long,
And the chance of withdrawal was zero

A skinny young woman of Broom
Took a candle alone in the gloom,
Now and then she would curse
When her lord, and his nurse
Made the bed in the neighbouring room

There was a rugby captain, a young man of upright life and modest bearing, an accountant by profession. He found the camp-followers flighty, over made-up and stupid, so he remained a bachelor.

One day in a bar he met a shapely girl who was cultured and intelligent, so he started dating her. One night she asked him to go back to her place, but when they entered the taxi, she gave a Park Lane address. The young man asked how a secretary could pay that sort of rent, and she told him that secretaries in London always took money from men, although seldom admitting it honestly.

He gave her all the money he had, begged her to reform, and fled the scene. When they later met by chance, she said: "Take me out to dinner, I've something to discuss." Over dinner she said:

"When I was 15, and home from school I found in my father's study a rare book he had smuggled in called 'Eastern Sexology'. I lay reading it, with my crotch drilling holes in the carpet, but father caught me, thrashed my bare bottom, and burned the book. I had read only one chapter, but I have never forgotten it, it was called the *Japanese Erotic*, and I have practised it to perfection, but never, I swear, with a man. I love you, take me home and I will do it for you." He eagerly agreed, but alas, the waiter handed him a telegram, his father was dying, he must go at once.

He asked around, but though the club knew lots about sex, they didn't know the *Japanese Erotic*, and told him to find out and report. But the girl had disappeared, and he searched in vain.

Months later she met him from work, and said she was washed up and repentant. If he would marry her she would reform, and make him a perfect wife. "And can I have the *Japanese Erotic*?" he asked. "Of course, darling, anything you like."

For various reasons the marriage was delayed, and she forgot the promise. On the wedding night he found her waiting naked on the bed, her full pink curves presenting a sexier sight than most men would ever witness.

"Rape me John, make me pregnant," and she opened her glorious thighs.

But he wanted *Japanese Erotic.*

She pressed up her splendid breasts: "Let me crush it between them."

He wanted *Japanese Erotic.*

She pointed to her blood-red mouth: "Put it in here as far as you like."

He wanted *Japanese Erotic.*

The girl smiled, slid gently off the bed, and bent down low over a chair, presenting to him a full round bottom of outstanding beauty.

"Darling," she said, "violate me any way you like, take your savage lust on me."

He wanted *Japanese Erotic.*

She straightened up, turned her liquid eyes to his, and still smiling, said:

"As my master commands; I am his slave. Go into the bathroom and cover yourself with lather, that's an essential part. As soon as I have got everything ready I will call you to come and slay me with your spear."

He could hardly contain himself. As soon as she "Cooeed" he rushed for the bathroom door, fell over the mat, hit his head on the pan, and died of concussion.

Shortly afterwards the girl died of a broken heart, and to this day not a living soul knows what *Japanese Erotic* is.

What is the difference between a Eunuch and an Eskimo?

A Eunuch is a massive vassal with a passive tassel.

An Eskimo is a rigid midget with a frigid digit.

* * *

What is the difference between an Opera Director and a baby?

A baby sucks his fingers.

* * *

What is the difference between a constipated owl and a bad marksman?

A bad marksman shoots and can't hit.

* * *

What is the difference between frustration and utter frustration?

Frustration is the first time you find you can't do it the second time.

Utter frustration is the second time you find you can't do it the first time.

Two into one won't go—true or false?
Yes, but only one at a time.

* * *

What is the definition of the true music lover?
A man who hears a lady singing in the bath and puts his *ear* to the keyhole.

* * *

What is the definition of old age?
When it takes all night to do what you used to do all night.

* * *

What is it that six men can do that three women can't?
Pee simultaneously in the same bucket.

* * *

HOW TO TELL CHARACTER FROM METHOD OF URINATION

Study this carefully, and determine your friend's character —and your own!

TYPE

Excitable: Pants twisted, can't find hole, rips in a rage.

Sociable: Joins friends in a pee whether he wants to or not, figures it costs nothing anyway.

Cross-eyed: Looks in stall on left, pees in one on right.

Timid: Can't go if anyone is looking. Pretends to, sneaks back later.

Aggressive: Whistles loudly, looks over to see how others are doing.

Indifferent: All stalls being occupied, calmly pisses in basin.

Clever sod: No hands. Adjusts tie. Gazes round for admiration.

Worried: Ex-serviceman, makes furtive but close examination.

Frivolous: Shoots a stream up and down and around. Has never really grown up.

Absentminded: Unbuttons waistcoat, takes out tie, pees in pants.

Disgruntled: Stands for a while, grunts, tries to fart, fails, walks out.

Sneaky: Lets strong silent farts whilst leaking.

Flashy: Tells loud jokes while leaking, shakes drops off with great flourish.

Sloppy: Tell-tale drops on flies. Never misses shoes. Walks out with flies undone. Adjusts balls 30 minutes later.

Childish: Pees directly into pool at bottom of stall. Enjoys the noise and splashing, interrupts to aim at a fly.

Patient: Stands there for hours on end.

Anxious: Leaves it late, wants to go so badly he can't start. Puts it back too soon, wetting leg. Adjusts flies in doorway.

Boastful: Stands back four feet and aims high up the wall. This type are invariably among the world's failures.

THIS IS TO CERTIFY THAT I, the undersigned, being a Female, about to enjoy sexual intercourse with . . . . . . am above the age of Consent. I am in my right mind, and not under the influence of any drink, drug or narcotic, neither does he have to use any kind of force, threat or promise, in order to influence me.

I FURTHER DECLARE that I am in no fear of him of whatsoever kind, that I do not expect him or want him to marry me, nor I to marry him. I do not know whether he is married or not, nor do I care. I am not asleep, or drunk and I enter into this relationship with him because I love it, and want it as much as he does.

UNDERTAKING I hereby undertake, provided I receive the satisfaction I have a right to expect, to play an early return engagement. Furthermore, I agree never to appear as a witness against him under the Bastardy Act, nor do I expect him to wear a contraceptive.

Signed, gladly of my own free will, and at the moment of slipping off my panties

. . . .

This . . . . day of . . . . . . 19 . . . .

Address. . . . .

. . . .

NUTS ON THE BALLS IN THE HALLS

There was an account in a Sunday paper about Friggington; which was said to be a place where bored housewives earned a bit on the side, or more improperly, on the back, and evening parties were held for "social sex". The disclosures were made by Councillor "Ginger" Nutt, a very prominent Liberal.

Alderman Sir John Stonehurst ("Stoney") Balls, leader of the Conservatives on the Council, disagreed: "These lies are all Nutt's," he said, "he's a singular fellow, no-one really knows where he hangs out."

"Nuts," said Nutt, "I am going to expose Balls, he wants to extend Tory spheres of influence, but the Conservative balls at the Town Hall are flopping, as anyone can see."

"I still say nothing is swinging in Friggington," replied Stoney Balls, and I am going to ask my brother, Canon Balls, to preach against the Liberals next Sunday. Everyone knows he bawls like a bull."

The last word was with Ginger Nutt: "The Canon is always shooting off in the pulpit, it doesn't produce any results; as for Stoney Balls, I'm going to keep tabs on him. Excuse me now though, I'm off to see the Rolling Stones."

Letter to the Woman's Monthly

Dear Aunt Fanny, Please can I have your advice as I am worried. I have started going serious with a nice young man of good family and with a good job. My mother is an actress and my father is always unemployed as well. My older sister is a model and my younger sister is also on the game. One of my uncles is a garage proprietor and he has a brother also a crook; my cousin is a male ballet dancer and several of his friends have also been convicted. I have a nephew and niece in jail for incest, and my Socialist brother-in-law is attending a VD Clinic.

Do you think I ought to confess to my fiancee that I am related to a Socialist?

Yours, Worried Winnie

TWO INTO ONE WON'T GO (EXCEPT ONE AT A TIME

There are about 25,000,000 females in this country
Of whom at least 12,000,000 are nubile
6,000,000 of them are married
The other 6,000,000 are single or widowed
Of these last, 4,000,000 like sex.
Add 6,000,000 to 4,000,000, that gives 10,000,000 taking sex
Assume 30% out of commission on any one evening
Gives 7,000,000 functioning fannies per night.

* * *

The average male, ignoring boasting and exaggeration
Is just over five inches when erect
Which, multiplied by 7,000,000 = 360,000,000 inches
Or ten million yards of sex per night!
This is between five and six hundred miles,
Multiplied by seven it is nearly 4,000 miles,
And four thousand miles a week, say 2,000,000 miles a year
Sure is a whole lot of sex.

ARE YOU GETTING YOUR SHARE?

Dear Sirs,

I took out what your agent called a "Comprehensive Policy" and he said if I ever suffered fire flood or theft or got struck by lightning I had only got to claim on you. I am a spinster living on my own, and I feel the cold so I had a man in to fix a wall heater. Yesterday, when I was adjusting a picture, the electric heater melted a big hole in the middle of my nylon dress, and I want to know if I am properly covered.

Yours tryly,
Virginia N. Rustyfann

Dear Miss Rustyfann,

We are sorry to hear about the hole in the front of your dress, and although it does not sound to us as if you are properly covered, we are sending our man at once to look into it. In any case, before he makes you an offer we have instructed him to find out what other cover you may have, and I should warn you that failure to disclose can lead to a breach, so we trust you will hide nothing.

Yours truly,
Commercial Union

Dear Sirs,

Reference the hole in the front of my dress, your man has looked into it, and is quite satisfied that I had no other cover. I must say, he came very quickly, and as he didn't want to offer much money he suggested that I let a piece in the front of the dress. After his expert attentions I shall need to let a piece into the front of my dress anyway. I must say he was very efficient, and offered to come again as often as I wanted.

However, I do not think I shall need this service again for some time, not unless I have the misfortune to sit on a hot stove that is!

Your satisfied customer
V. Nomora Rustyfann

HOW SOON ARE YOU GOING TO FOCUS?

SCENE : *The house of a childless couple, married five years.*

Husband : Well dear, I must be off to work, but don't forget, the "Artificial Insemination" expert is coming this morning.

Wife : Darling, do you think we did the right thing?

H : Of course my dear. You want a child, I want a child, we don't want to adopt, so this is the only way.

W. I hope he doesn't want to do anything to me, I'm not a bit in the mood.

H : Oh you great big silly! He only wants to talk; the action's weeks away. (*He kisses her and departs.*)

There is a loud knock on the door

W : Ooh, good morning, are you the gentleman from . . .?

MAN: Yes, that's right, I've come about the baby. (*Thinks to himself, so this IS the right house. Why the hell can't they bring their babies to the studio to be photographed?*)

W : Won't you take your coat off and put your bag down Mr . . . ?

M : Jones. I hope this is a convenient time. Your husband's at work I presume?

W : Naturally. He wouldn't want to be around as he's not going to do it himself, even though he is mad keen on babies.

M : Quite quite. Takes a professional touch to get results. I suggest two on the settee, two on the mat, and one or two naked on the bed. That'll need a fairly long exposure.

W: (*Alarmed*) You're not going to do it *now?* I thought this was to discuss it!

M: Madam your husband placed a firm order and paid. I don't want to come more than is necessary. Half a dozen shots now, and one is sure to produce an attractive baby. I'm a busy man, I've got two more to do this morning.

W: Two more to do this morning!

M: Yes, a model wants to try various positions in a topless dress. She wants an enlargement for advertising purposes. Afterwards some nuns want me to take them in a group on their knees, part of a religious festival, I gather.

W: You do get around, don't you.

M: Yes indeed, variety is the spice of my job. Want to see some samples (*produces photos of babies*), here's a good one, I got it on top of a moving bus. Mother a film actress, divorced, but wanted one for publicity. I only had the chance of one shot too.

W: Only one shot?

M: Every time the bus turned a corner she rolled off the seat. Here's a good one, I did that in Hyde Park when the snow was on the ground, the ducks kept pecking my equipment.

W: Ooh goodness, there's twins!

M: Ah yes, that was sensational. On the front at Brighton, crowds gathered round, the mother was so pleased and excited she paid me double.

W: I think perhaps we'd better get on with it.

M : Of course, I'm ready when you are, just let me get my tackle ready.

W : But, isn't it?

M : Yes, I mean, I just have to get it out, you see I always reckon to get the best results with a three foot stand . . . my gord, she's fainted !

Dancing is the vertical expression of horizontal intention.

* * *

Virtue is insufficient temptation.

* * *

A camel is a horse designed by a committee.

* * *

Wife: If you really loved me, you would have married someone else.

* * *

Rear view of any girl in jeans = Two ferrets fighting in a sack.

* * *

A wife = A woman who can turn an old rake into a lawn mower.

* * *

It is easy for a girl to stay on the straight and narrow, if she's built that way.

* * *

Big Ben, to the Leaning Tower : I've got the time if you've got the inclination.

*   *   *

A doctor was asked to address a crowded meeting on sex. He rose, said : "It gives me great pleasure" and sat down.

*   *   *

Mummy, Mummy, why can't we give our Alice's baby a proper funeral? Oh, shut up child, and keep pulling the chain.

*   *   *

Driving Instructor to Vicar (who has just felled a lamp-post) : "Here endeth the first lesson !"

*   *   *

Report of Camera Club : Our President has produced remarkable results from a 16 year old Brownie.

*   *   *

There is now on offer a gadget you can screw on the bed and it does all the housework. It is called a wife.

*   *   *

A clever typist = One who never misses a period.

*   *   *

A smart secretary : She wears mink by day and fox by night.

*   *   *

Granddaughter (16) Tell me about the men in your life?
Grandma (75) My dear, it isn't the men in your life it's the life in your men that's important.

A schoolgirl who reached adolescence
Asked : What did they mean by pubescence?
Said the Vicar : A dame
And a man, aren't the same,
And he widened the split with the difference!

Said a crafty old doctor named Hammon
Im*pote*nce is getting too common.
Pills, oysters, and honey
Are sheer waste of money,
What works, is to bed a fresh woman.

There was a young lady named Bickers
Whose cousin came off in her knickers,
A tadpole in cream
Found a split through a seam
And they had to rush round to the Vicar's.

There was a young lady named Lees
Whose titties resembled two peas,
Yet she had such technique
She could stiffen the weak,
And leave all the strong on their knees

A "teaser" in spite of all rumours
Would only have sex in her bloomers,
A rigger named Hussett
Drilled right through the gusset
And tapped her for future consumers.

He had been a most eligible bachelor, but now he was on his way to get married. As luck would have it, his car was involved in an accident, and a thorough examination revealed only a ligament laceration in a most intimate place. Despite his protestations, the doctor insisted on putting a splint on it, consisting mainly of four small strips of narrow wood bound together.

When the groom and his bride were alone in their boudoir that night she proceeded to disrobe in a most provocative manner. When she unveiled her shoulders she said, "Look, Dear, never been touched by any man."

Then she stripped to the waist and said, "Look, darling, no other man's eyes have ever gazed upon these." She continued this routine until finally the groom could contain himself no longer. Indicating his damaged organ, he said, "That's nothing. Look at this . . . still in the original crate !"

NIFTY THINKING

A woman walked into a very busy butcher's shop. Looking at the meats and poultry on display, she suddenly grabbed hold of a dressed chicken. She picked up one wing, sniffed it; picked up the other wing, sniffed it; picked up one leg, sniffed it; picked up the other leg, sniffed it. Just as she finished sniffing the second leg, the butcher walked up to her and said, "Madam, could *you* pass such a test?"

I SPY

There was once a playboy who had the reputation of winding up under the table every time he went to a night club with a pretty girl. Not drunk, you understand . . . just an insatiable curiosity.

And today's story has a vicar alone on the first tee. He sees a fellow standing there and suggests they play together. After a couple of holes, the stranger tells the minister what he's doing wrong. As they play along, the vicar gets more advice, all of it good. The man of the cloth finishes the round six strokes under his usual score. He thanks his golf partner and the fellow says: "That will be £25. I'm the pro here." The vicar argues but to no avail. So he tells the pro to drop over to the rectory that evening to collect his fee. "And when you come," suggests the vicar, "bring your mother and father. I'll marry them at the same time!"

BUTTONS UP

The teacher took her class of little boys and girls on an outing, near a race track. As the children left the bus, several of them had to answer the call of nature.

Naturally, the teacher helped them.

She was helping one very cute little fellow when he said: "Please miss, would you mind letting me button my own pants? I'm in a terrible hurry . . . I have to get to the track in time to ride in the third race."

FULL MARKS

Diana lay sprawled in sweet exhaustion on the bed, her attire consisting of one earring. Beside her, Bob wore nothing at all. He slowly lit two cigarettes and passed one to Diana. For a long moment, smoke and silence hung in the air, then: "My mother always told me to be good," Diana said with a little smile. "Was I?"

THE HARD STUFF

The most notorious tippler in an Irish village, making his way unsteadily homeward, encountered the parish priest who inquired about the suspicious bulge in his coat pocket.

"It's holy water, Father," the culprit protested piously.

The priest removed the bottle, sniffed at it and announced that it contained whiskey.

"Glory be," cried the drunk. "A miracle!"

MARITAL BLISS

Marriage is the process of finding out what kind of man your wife would have preferred.

SMELLBOUND

A spirited session of poker was in progress as a new arrival, a practical joker, proceeded to spray the nearest player with the contents of a perfume atomizer.

"Hey, don't spray that on me," the player shouted, "my wife will think I spent the evening in a brothel!"

The player sitting next to him said, "You can squirt me if you like. My wife was never in a brothel and she won't recognize the smell."

SMALL TALK

The wife was understandably furious when she came home unexpectedly and found her husband in bed with a lady midget.

"You promised me two weeks ago that you would never cheat on me again," she stormed.

Her husband shrugged nonchalantly. "Take it easy, dear," he said airily. "Can't you see I'm tapering off? !"

MIXED EMOTIONS

Watching your mother-in-law drive over a cliff in your brand new Jaguar.

COLD SHOULDER

The husband leaned over to his wife and asked, "Come on, darling, let's make love."

His wife replied, "George, I wish you wouldn't talk that way; the children might hear you. Whenever you're in the mood, why don't you say to me, 'Honey, I'd like to use your washing machine'."

A few nights later, the wife felt in a romantic mood and leaning over to her husband, asked, "George, would you like to use my washing machine?" George replied, "To tell you the truth, dear, it was just a small bundle. I did it by hand."

WHICH WITCH?

Once upon a time there was a beautiful young girl taking a stroll through the woods. All at once she saw an extremely ugly bull frog seated on a log and to her amazement the bull frog spoke to her.

"Maiden," croaked the frog, "would you do me a big favour? This will be hard for you to believe, but I was once a handsome, charming prince and then a mean, ugly old witch cast a spell over me and turned me into a frog."

"Oh, what a pity!" exclaimed the pretty girl. "I'll do anything I can to help you break such a spell."

"Well, Miss," replied the frog, "the only way that this spell can be taken off and I can be returned to a handsome young man again is for some lovely and pretty young girl to take me home and let me spend the night under her pillow."

The young girl took the ugly frog home and placed him beneath her pillow that night when she retired. When she awoke the next morning, sure enough, there beside her in the bed was a very young, handsome man, and plainly of royal blood.

And so they lived happily ever after, except that until this day her father and mother still do not believe her story.

BUSINESS AS USUAL

A doctor in London for a medical convention was conversing with a gorgeous blonde in the lobby of the Ritz when his wife suddenly emerged from the lift. Eyeing the departing figure, the wife snapped, "How do you happen to know her?"

"Oh, just professionally," the doctor replied.

The wife raised a sarcastic eyebrow. "Yours, or hers?" she asked.

TIDYING UP

The shapely young nurse was walking down the hospital corridor with her uniform askew and part of her bosom showing when she encountered the matron. The matron bawled her out for improper dress and shameful display of her body.

Straightening her clothes in confusion, the young nurse blurted the excuse, "I'm terribly sorry but you know those damned interns never put anything away!"

CORRESPONDENT

Blonde: "I've been receiving threatening letters in the mail—isn't that against the law?"

Lawyer: "Why yes, who has been writing them?"

Blonde: "My lover's wife."

DRUM MAJOR

She had her suspicions for a long time, but when he arrived home late one night with signs of lipstick on his cheek, she decided it was time to speak.

"Now look here, Reggie," she complained, "I'll have you know once and for all that I will not play second fiddle!"

"Sec'n fiddle!" he shrieked, "Sec'n fiddle! You can take it from me, Evelyn, you're damn lucky to be in the ruddy band at all!"

MONKEY GLANDS

Two old men meet on a corner.

First old man: "Where have you been for the past eight weeks?"

Second old man: "In jail."

First old man: "You in jail? How come?"

Second old man: "Well, about eight weeks ago I was standing on a corner, and this beautiful young girl rushes up with a policeman and says, 'He's the man, officer. He's the one who attacked me.' I tell you, I felt so flattered, I admitted it."

THE RED LIGHT

Two sailors were walking down the street in a strange town when a girl stuck her head out of a doorway and shouted: "Come in, fellows, and I'll give you something you've never had before." One sailor looked at the other and said: "Run like hell. She's got leprosy."

ON PROBATION

"Send me the bookkeeper," roared the senior partner.

"Listen you," he bellowed when the bookkeeper appeared. "I can't stand for too much more of this. Last year you forged three cheques in my name, six months ago you stole thousands of pounds. I discovered you were disclosing our business secrets and several nights ago you took advantage of my daughter. Now, I'm warning you—the next least little thing you do, out you go!"

AS NATURE INTENDED

The young girl had not been feeling well and went to her family doctor. "Young lady," said the doctor, "you're pregnant." "But that can't be. The only men I've been with are nudists and in our colony we practise sex only with our eyes." "Well, my dear," said the doctor, "someone in that colony is cockeyed."

LEONARD ROSSITER

THE LOWEST FORM OF WIT

Sarcasm is the lowest form of wit – no one is beneath using it – but it is also the most satisfying. There is no greater pleasure than pinning your squirming victim to the dinner-table with a carefully sharpened and coolly aimed insult or flooring him with a sudden and crippling kick beneath the belt.

Sarcasm requires deadly accuracy and perfect timing. It is the most skilful kind of unarmed combat and because no holds are barred it is also the most dangerous. THE LOWEST FORM OF WIT is a complete handbook for aspiring masters and mistresses of sarcasm compiled by Leonard Rossiter, a black belt of this vicious art. He tells you everything you need to know about sarcasm from its low-down role in history to specific advice on dealing with traffic wardens, bank managers, neighbours, foreigners and other despicable persons.

This is a treasury of biting jibes and stinging retorts which explores the lowest kind of wit in the highest kind of style.

HUMOUR 0 7221 7513 2 £2.75

A THOROUGHLY LEWD COLLECTION OF EXCEEDINGLY RUDE RHYMES!!

BAWDY Limericks

Ribald, ingenious, hilariously blue – this side-splitting selection of bawdy limericks will have you reeling with riotous laughter and mirth-filled merriment. There's Adam complacently stroking his madam . . . Irene who made an offering quite obscene . . . Hyde who fell down a privy and died . . . the young fellow of Kent who had a peculiar bent . . . the brainy professor named Zed who dreamed of a buxom co-ed . . . and many, many more!

0 7221 1297 1 HUMOUR £1.95

SHEATH-BURSTING ROMANCE!!!

BRUTE!

MALCOLM BENNETT & AIDAN HUGHES

BRUTE!
Colossal, work-hardened men! Wild untameable women! Savage, unbridled passion! Raw and erotic tales of gut-wrenching drama and suspense!!

BRUTE!
Romance, cruelty and religion! Sport, crime and agriculture! Horror, western and football!!

BRUTE!
The cult comic of the 80s now unleashed in paperback!

'Unmatched in contemporary British comic art'
CITY LIMITS

'Tough and dirty' THE FACE

'Graphic, gruesome and hilarious' BLITZ

'In future all novels will be written like this' TIME OUT

0 7221 1565 2 CULT/GENERAL FICTION £1.95